A Con
Introdu
to Sa

OTHER TITLES OF INTEREST

A Concise Introduction to Sage

by
D. Weale

BERNARD BABANI (publishing) LTD
THE GRAMPIANS
SHEPHERDS BUSH ROAD
LONDON W6 7NF
ENGLAND

PLEASE NOTE

Although every care has been taken with the production of this book to ensure that any projects, designs, modifications and/or programs, etc., contained herewith, operate in a correct and safe manner and also that any components specified are normally available in Great Britain, the Publishers and Author do not accept any responsibility in any way for the failure, including fault in design, of any project, design, modification or program to work correctly or to cause damage to any other equipment that it may be connected to or used in conjunction with, or in respect of any other damage or injury that may be so caused, nor do the Publishers accept responsibility in any way for the failure to obtain specified components.

Notice is hereby also given that if any equipment that is still under warranty is modified in any way or used or connected with home-built equipment then that warranty may be void.

© 1991 BERNARD BABANI (publishing) LTD

First Published — October 1991

British Library Cataloguing in Publication Data:
Weale, David
    An Introduction to Sage.
    I. Title
    657.02855369

ISBN 0 85934 258 1

Typeset direct from disk by EMSET, London NW10
Printed and Bound in Great Britain by Cox & Wyman Ltd, Reading

ABOUT THE AUTHOR

David Weale is a fellow of the Institute of Chartered Accountants and has worked in university administration and chartered accountancy practices (dealing mainly with small businesses). At present he is a full-time lecturer in further education at Yeovil Tertiary College where he lectures in business computing. He also runs and has been known to enter triathlons as a relaxation from computing.

He is married with three children and a Siamese cat and lives in Somerset.

TRADEMARKS

DEDICATION

To all my family and especially to my father, without whose guidance earlier in my life, this book would not have been written.

CONTENTS

INTRODUCTION

Sage is an accounting program which comes in several versions from Sage Bookkeeper to Sage Financial Controller. The simplest version is Sage Bookkeeper and the one with the most features is Sage Financial Controller (which contains features many small businesses will not need).

This book is intended to explain how to begin to use Sage by using examples of data and explaining how the data is entered into Sage and the results of this data entry.

The reader will learn most effectively not by merely reading the book but by actually using the program and entering the data from the book (the book explains how to do this using step by step instructions). This will enable you to practice using Sage and to get used to the program before entering *real* data. The data used is for the retailer of sports shoes called Fast Feet but the ideas could apply to any business.

The practice data can be cleared from the system after use and the real data can then be entered (or more practice can take place until the reader is confident in his/her use of the program)

It is assumed that the reader has had Sage installed on their computer and that they are familiar with the operation of their particular PC.

Obviously every facet of Sage cannot be covered in a book of this size, but once the reader has grasped the essentials then it is relatively easy to use the rest of your version of Sage.

Sage will run on all IBM PC's, however unless you have a hard disk, there are limitations on which version of Sage you can use, and what you can do with it. I would suggest that it is sensible to use a PC with a hard disk for both the flexibility and speed of working. For specific information read the Sage Installation Guide or contact your dealer.

The System Date
To get the most from the exercises, it is best to reset the system date for each section of the manual. This is so that the illustrations will be similar to your printouts (although this is not material as long as you are aware that on occasion you may have slightly different figures to the book)
To reset the system date simply exit to the DOS prompt, type Date and enter the required date.
Set the system date now for 300691

The Ledgers

Every business using Sage will use ledgers so we will begin at that stage.

There are three ledgers used in accounting:

The Sales Ledger
The Purchase Ledger
The Nominal Ledger

Each of these has a different purpose which will be explained.

Getting Into The Program

The first screen that appears is the date, if this is correct then press **RETURN** and type the password

LETMEIN

followed by **RETURN**

The first screen should look like this

Sage Menu Program	FAST FEET	30th June 1991

Sales Ledger
Purchase Ledger
Nominal Ledger
Payroll
Stock Control
Sales Order Processing
Purchase Order Processing
Report Generator
Utilities

Quit

Function Keys

It is worthwhile making a note of the function keys available within the Sage program.

F1	help
F2	displays the calculator (press ESC to remove it)
F5	current day's date
F6	repeats the previous line
F8	clears the entry in a field
Shift F6	increments the previous field
CTRL together with arrow key moves the cursor across fields when entering or editing data.	

Note:
If you want to take backups of your files onto floppy discs at any time (for example at the end of a session), look at the section on Backing Up and Restoring your data.

THE SALES LEDGER

The Sales Ledger is used to record Invoices sent to customers and the money received from the customers in payment for the goods.

Each customer is given its own account in the sales ledger, and there will be as many sales ledger accounts as there are customers.

The balance on each account is the amount owing to your firm by the customer, and the total of all the balances of all the customer accounts is the total amount due to the firm (often called the *Debtors* figure)

Setting Up The Sales Ledger
Before you can actually use the Sage program, there is a certain amount of preparatory work to be done in setting up the ledgers so that data can be entered.

The first task is to set up the names and addresses of the customers you intend to deal with (*always remember that these can be added to or altered whenever necessary*)

The details to be filled in are:

a) Reference (a code or short name is normally entered preferably something easy to remember), up to six characters can be used.

b) The Name and Address.

c) Other information that can be entered includes:
   i) Credit Limit.
   ii) Turnover.
   iii) Telephone number.
   iv) Contact name.

To enter the customer details

From the MAIN menu select

SALES LEDGER   use the cursor keys or type the first character of the word and then
               RETURN (but make sure that the correct option has been chosen
               as on some menus there are several options beginning with the
               same letter)

the screen should then look like this:

Financial Controller	Sales Ledger	30th June 1991

No. of entries : 0

Customer Details	Address List
Batched Data Entry	Account Balances (Aged)
Invoice Production	Transaction History
Receipts	Day Books
Refunds	Statements
Contra Entries	Letters
Bad Debt Write Off	

then select

CUSTOMER DETAILS

The screen should now look like this:

Financial Controller	Customer Details	30th June 1991

```
                Account Reference :

                  Account Name :
                       Address :
                         ..    :
                         ..    :
                         ..    :
                   Credit Limit :
                      Turnover :

                Telephone No. :
                 Contact Name :
                 Discount Code :
                 Analysis Code :
```

Follow the prompts and enter the following account references, account names and addresses:

After entering the A/C reference you need to press the Y key to open a new account

It is important to hit the **RETURN** key after every line (including the last line of each address) otherwise the whole address may not be recorded.

As each account is completed press **ESC** and **POST**, then continue onto the next entry, remember to read it through first.

ABLE
The Able Athletic Club
The Council Track
Yeovil
Somerset
BA21 6RD

HOPE
The Hopeful Hobblers
The Grange
Ilchester
Somerset
BA34 9GF

SLOW
The Slow Sloggers
Packard
The Main Street
Blandford Forum, Dorset
BL12 5EW

TROT
The Trotters
34 Upper Town Road
Dorchester
Dorset
DO21 7GH

After entering these, whenever an account needs looking at, you only need to use the short reference (which is why it is helpful to choose a short and easily remembered reference)

When finished, **RETURN** to the SALES LEDGER menu by pressing **ESC** after having **POSTED** the final entry (at this point there should be a blank entry form displayed on the screen).

You should have now returned to the SALES LEDGER menu

You can now examine what you have entered by selecting:

ADDRESS LIST

Follow through the questions on the screen, pressing **RETURN** on each one; there is no need to enter any data.

Your screen will look like this:

Financial Controller		Address List		30th June 1991
Ref.	Account Name		Ref.	Account Name
ABLE	The Able Athletic Club		HOPE	The Hopeful Hobblers
SLOW	The Slow Joggers		TROT	The Trotters
	Press ESC to finish, RETURN to continue			

When finished **ESC** and **ESC** again to get back to the original menu.

Entering Opening Balances For The Sales Ledger
It is assumed for the purpose of the book that your firm has been in existence for some time and has been using a manual system to record its accounts. However if you are beginning business for the first time then obviously there will be no opening balances to enter.

After entering the names and addresses for your customers, you can enter the balances on each sales ledger account that existed at the time you begin the computerised accounting system (normally this is done at the start of a month and the balances to be entered will be those at the end of the previous month).

To enter the opening balances

From the MAIN menu Choose:

SALES LEDGER

then

BATCHED DATA ENTRY

then

SALES INVOICES

9

The screen should look like this:

Financial Controller	Sales Invoices	30th June 1991

A/C Name :   Tax Rate :

N/C Name :   Batch Total :   0.00

A/C Date Inv. N/C Dep. Details   Nett Amnt Tc Tax Amnt

                                       00.00   0.00

Notes:

A/C	is the account reference for the customer.
DATE	is the invoice date. (for the purpose of this exercise date as 310591)
Inv	is the invoice code
N/C	for opening balances this will be 9998 (Suspense Account)
Nett	this MUST be the GROSS amount on the invoice (as there is no tax element in the opening balances).
Tc	there is no tax so use the code T9.
Tax	this should be zero.

Now enter the following opening sales balances which were outstanding when you begin your computerised accounting:

A/C	Date	Inv.	N/C	Details	Nett Amnt	Tc	Tax Amnt
ABLE	310591	111	9998	30 Nike Pegasus	910.56	T9	0.00
TROT	310591	131	9998	15 pairs socks	25.69	T9	0.00
HOPE	310591	165	9998	5 Club Vests	48.32	T9	0.00
					984.57		0.00

Use F6 to repeat the previous line (this can save a considerable amount of time)

In this exercise no Department is allocated so RETURN for this entry.

Note how entering the account reference brings up the full account name.

When finished **ESC** and **POST** the entries and then **ESC** (three times) back to the MAIN menu.

THE PURCHASE LEDGER

Setting Up The Purchase Ledger

The Purchase ledger is in a sense a mirror image of the Sales ledger, it is used to record the purchases you make, the names of the suppliers you buy them from and the money you pay to those suppliers.

The balance on each supplier's account is the difference between the invoices you have received from those suppliers and the money you have paid to them.

The total of all the balances for all the suppliers is the total amount you owe at that point in time and the ledger is often called the *creditors* ledger.

To enter the suppliers' names

From the MAIN menu select

PURCHASE LEDGER

From this menu select

SUPPLIER DETAILS

Now create the following supplier accounts in the same way as you used in the Sales ledger (remember to **ESC** and **POST** after each supplier's details have been entered)

The details to be entered are the account reference,the account name and the address.

ASICS	Olympian Sports UK Ltd	FAST	Fastrack
	Moorfield Industrial Est		Leeds Rd
	Yeadon		Ilkley
	Leeds		West Yorks
	LS19 7BN		LE23 8GF
OAK	Oakley	RON	Ron Hill Sports
	Serval Marketing		PO Box 11
	Clifton Road		Hyde
	Shefford, Berks		Cheshire
	SG17 5AE		SK14 1RD
SWE	The Sweat Shop		
	33 Broad Street		
	Teddington		
	Mddx		
	TW11 8QZ		

When finished entering all the details, **ESC ESC** back to the main menu.

Then look at the purchase accounts (to check them) by selecting from the MAIN menu:

PURCHASE LEDGER

and then

ADDRESS LIST

Press **RETURN** through the questions except for Name & Address where you should enter A (for all).

This will display all the names and addresses you have entered.

When finished **ESC ESC** back to the main menu.

After having entered the names and addresses of the suppliers, the balances on their accounts (derived from the manual records) can be entered.

From the MAIN menu select:

PURCHASE LEDGER

then

BATCHED DATA ENTRY

then

PURCHASE INVOICES

Entries follow the same form as for the sales opening balances.

Enter the following purchase ledger opening balance:

A/C	Date	Inv.	N/C	Dep.	Details	Nett Amnt	Tc	Tax Amnt
ASICS	310591	a3456	9998	0	20 pairs shoes	550.00	T9	0.00
OAK	310591	x3122	9998	0	10 sunglasses	430.23	T9	0.00
FAST	310591	f798	9998	0	50 club vests	250.56	T9	0.00
RON	310591	8769	9998	0	120 prs tracksters	734.12	T9	0.00
						1964.91		0.00

ESC and POST the entries.

Then ESC (three times) back to the main menu

THE NOMINAL LEDGER

Setting Up The Nominal Ledger
This ledger is somewhat different to the Sales and Purchase ledgers; it is used to record income and expenditure.

The figures from the Sales and Purchase ledgers are automatically recorded in the Nominal ledger and are analysed by their *Nominal* code.

When items are entered into the Sales or Purchase ledger they are allocated a nominal code. There can be as many nominal codes as you require for your business.

For example
Motor car expenses could be analysed into several nominal codes (perhaps motor tax, petrol, services, etc.).

You can analyse the income and expenditure in as much (or as little) detail as you wish, it all depends upon how much information you require from your accounts and ledgers.

The Nominal ledger is also used to record income and expenditure that do not go through the sales or purchase ledgers, e.g. standing orders, cash payments, etc.

From the Nominal Ledger a trial balance is produced, this is a list of the balances on all the ledger accounts. It is used to produce the profit & loss account and the balance sheet.

Setting Up The Nominal Ledger as follows.
From the MAIN menu select:

NOMINAL LEDGER

then

NOMINAL ACCOUNT STRUCTURE

then

ACCOUNT NAMES

The screen will look like this:

Financial Controller	Nominal Account Structure	30th June 1991

```
            Account Reference :
              Account Name :
              Yearly Budget :

        Month 1 :                    Month 7 :
        Month 2 :                    Month 8 :
        Month 3 :                    Month 9 :
        Month 4 :                    Month 10 :
        Month 5 :                    Month 11 :
        Month 6 :                    Month 12 :
```

Please enter the following (enter reference number and account name only):

Remember to ESC and POST after each entry:
Depending upon which version of Sage you have, some of these accounts exist.
Remember if you have to alter any, **F8** removes the existing name.

16

Ref	A/C Name	Ref	A/C Name
0011	Leasehold property	0030	Office equipment
0040	Furniture & fixtures	1001	Stock
1100	Debtors control account	1200	Bank current Account
1230	Petty cash	2100	Creditors control account
2200	Tax control account	2201	VAT liability
2210	PAYE	2211	National insurance
3100	Reserves	3200	Profit & loss account
4000	Shoe sales	4001	Clothing sales
4002	Equipment sales	4003	Miscellaneous sales
4905	Distribution & carriage	5000	Shoe purchases
5001	Clothing purchases	5002	Equipment purchases
5003	Miscellaneous	5200	Opening stock
5201	Closing stock	6201	Advertising
7100	Rent	7102	Water rates
7103	General rates	7104	Premises insurance
7200	Electricity	7300	Fuel & oil
7301	Repairs & servicing	7303	Vehicle insurance
7304	Misc motor exps	7501	Postage & carriage
7502	Telephone	7601	Audit & accountancy
7603	Professional fees	7901	Bank charges
9998	Suspense account		

You can see from this list the accounts that are being set up for the firm in this example. Sage has many preset (default) account names which can be printed out by selecting the NOMINAL LEDGER and ACCOUNTS LIST.

ESC (twice) back to the NOMINAL LEDGER

Look at the opening Trial Balance by selecting:

TRIAL BALANCE and **RETURN** through the questions.

This displays the trial balance showing the figures you have entered for the Sales and Purchase ledgers, and the Suspense Account.

Financial Controller	Trial Balance		30th June 1991
Ref.	Accounts Name	Debit	Credit
1100	DEBTORS CONTROL ACCOUNT	984.57	
2100	CREDITORS CONTROL ACCOUNT		1964.91
9998	SUSPENSE ACCOUNT	980.34	
		1964.91	1964.91

Press ESC to finish, RETURN to continue

As can be seen there are balances on the Debtors and Creditors Control Accounts and the Suspense Account.

These need to be zeroed to remove the suspense account balance (although the individual amounts owing and due to the firm are still held in the individual sales and purchase accounts)

To do this first take a note of the balances on the accounts and then **ESC** back to the NOMINAL LEDGER menu select:

JOURNAL ENTRIES

This is the only aspect of Sage for which a knowledge of double entry is really necessary, although an understanding of double entry is useful for a complete understanding of accountancy and what the figures and reports represent.

Post the opposite entries i.e if the original was a debit entry, then the journal will be a credit for the same amount.

If nothing is to be entered in a field then the RETURN key can be used.

The entries should be:

Financial Controller		Journal Entries			30th June 1991

Date :310591   Reference :
N/C Name :   Batch Total :   -0.00

N/C	Dep.	Details	Tc	Debit	Credit
1100	0	o/bal	T9		984.57
2100	0	o/bal	T9	1964.91	
9998	0	o/bal	T9		980.34

Batch Total MUST be ZERO before exit

ESC and **POST** the completed journal.

Then **ESC** back to the NOMINAL LEDGER menu.

After doing this, check that it has been successful by trying to display the trial balance again, if it does not display then there are no balances and the correct journal entries have been made.

THE OPENING TRIAL BALANCE

After clearing the debtors, creditors and suspense balances from the trial balance so that you can start with zero balances, then enter the following details to reflect the correct position at the start of your computerised accounts:

In the example the opening balances are:

Office Equipment	£2400.00
Furniture & fittings	£1200.00
Stock	£ 769.43
Amounts owed to us	£ 984.57
Amounts we owe to suppliers	£1964.91
Bank current account	£ 768.54
Petty cash	£ 7.98
Reserves (our capital)	£4165.61

To do this.

From the MAIN menu select:

NOMINAL LEDGER

then

JOURNAL ENTRIES

Then enter the following information remembering the key **F6** repeats the previous line.

Financial Controller			Journal Entries		30th June 1991

Date :310591 Reference :
N/C Name : Batch Total : -0.00

N/C	Dep.	Details	Tc	Debit	Credit
0030	0	o/bal	T9	2400.00	
0040	0	o/bal	T9	1200.00	
1001	0	o/bal	T9	769.43	
1100	0	o/bal	T9	984.57	
2100	0	o/bal	T9		1964.91
1200	0	o/bal	T9	768.54	
1230	0	o/bal	T9	7.98	
3100	0	o/bal	T9		4165.61

Batch Total MUST be ZERO before exit

Notes

If you make a mistake then move the cursor back, enter the new figure and RETURN.

ESC and **POST** these entries and then **ESC** back to the NOMINAL LEDGER menu.

To check the opening Trial Balance select:

TRIAL BALANCE

and **RETURN** through the questions. This displays the trial balance showing the figures you have just entered.

The trial balance looks like this:

Financial Controller	Trial Balance		30th June 1991
Ref.	Accounts Name	Debit	Credit
0030	OFFICE EQUIPMENT	2400.00	
0040	FURNITURE AND FIXTURES	1200.00	
1001	STOCK	769.43	
1100	DEBTORS CONTROL ACCOUNT	984.57	
1200	BANK CURRENT ACCOUNT	768.54	
1.230	PETTY CASH	7.98	
2100	CREDITORS CONTROL ACCOUNT		1964.91
3100	RESERVES		4165.61
		6130.52	6130.52

Press ESC to finish, RETURN to continue

ESC back to the NOMINAL LEDGER menu.

Looking At The Data Entered
You can look at the data you have entered as follows:

Transactions

From the NOMINAL LEDGER menu choose:

TRANSACTION HISTORY

then **RETURN** through the questions.

This displays a history of all the transactions that have taken place in each of the nominal accounts.

Sales account history

ESC back to the MAIN menu and choose:

SALES LEDGER

then

ACCOUNT BALANCES (Aged)

then **RETURN** through the questions. Use the right arrow key to see the aged display (as shown at the bottom of the screen).

This will have given you familiarity with some the reports that can be accessed using Sage.

ESC back to the MAIN menu.

So far.

You have learned how to set up the ledgers, how to enter opening balances into the ledger accounts, how to carry out journal entries and how to produce a trial balance showing the balances in each account.

Now you are going to look at how to enter the day to day transactions of the business into the ledger accounts.

POSTING TRANSACTIONS INTO THE LEDGERS

After the ledgers have been set up and the opening balances (if your firm has been trading before setting up the computerised accounts) have been entered, then the day to day transactions can begin to be entered into the ledgers.

Sales

Select

SALES LEDGER

then

BATCHED DATA ENTRY

then

SALES INVOICES

Enter the following data from invoices you have sent to customers

(watch how after entering the A/C code, the A/C Name will automatically appear in the section above)

Notes:
Remember to use **F6** to repeat the previous line, and **F5** to print todays date.
Shift + **F6** increments the invoice number by one.
Watch how the calculation of the VAT is automatic after the entry of the correct VAT code.

A/C	Date	Inv.	N/C	Dep.	Details	Nett Amnt	Tc	Tax Amnt
SLOW	070691	300	4000	0	5 prs asics shoes	200.00	T1	35.00
HOPE	090691	301	4001	0	10 club vests	80.00	T1	14.00
HOPE	090691	301	4000	0	10 prs asics shoes	400.00	T1	70.00
TROT	100691	302	4001	0	5 oakley sunglasses	300.00	T1	52.50
ABLE	100691	303	4001	0	20 club vests	160.00	T1	28.00
SLOW	160691	304	4000	0	10 prs NB shoes	450.00	T1	78.75
						1590.00		278.25

Check for mistakes. Use the cursor keys to move about, then re-enter the correct details.

Check again. When all is correct press **ESC** then **POST** the transaction details.

Always check before the final **POST**ing. Mistakes are easier to correct before **POST**ing.

Then **ESC** (three times) back to the MAIN menu.

After the SALES LEDGER you can enter transactions into the PURCHASE LEDGER

Purchases

Select

PURCHASE LEDGER

then

BATCHED DATA ENTRY

then

PURCHASE INVOICES

Enter the following data from your suppliers' invoices:

A/C	Date	Inv.	N/C	Dep.	Details	Nett Amnt	Tc	Tax Amnt
SWE	020691	ff456	5000	0	25 prs NB shoes	775.00	T1	135.63
ASICS	020691	dd4563	5000	0	20 prs asics shoes	575.00	T1	100.63
OAK	050691	42134	5001	0	40 prs sunglasses	1700.32	T1	297.56
FAST	070691	s234	5002	0	10 prs watches	55.00	T1	9.63
FAST	090691	s235	5001	0	50 club vests	225.00	T1	39.38
SWE	160691	ff569	5000	0	5 prs nike shoes	122.89	T1	21.51
FAST	160691	s345	5002	0	10 bumbags	45.00	T1	7.88
						3498.21		612.22

After entering the above transactions

ESC and **POST**

then

ESC (three times) to RETURN to the MAIN menu.

This has dealt with entering invoices into the sales and purchase ledgers, now you can learn how to enter Payments and Receipts in these ledgers.

Choose

SALES LEDGER then

RECEIPTS

After raising invoices to your customers they will eventually be paid. You will have paid these cheques into your bank and now you need to enter the details in your sales ledger to clear the invoices.

A list of these payments is shown below:

A/C	Date	Ref.	Nett Amnt
ABLE	020691	0	910.56
HOPE	120691	0	612.32
TROT	160691	0	25.69

> The nominal code is 1200 for all the transactions

RETURN on the N/C Bank (this should be 1200).

Enter the first of the above transactions.

After doing so the screen will look like this:

Financial Controller				Receipts		30th June 1991	

N/C Bank   : 1200   N/C Bank Name :   BANK CURRENT ACCOUNT
A/C Ref.   : ABLE   A/C Name   :   The Able Athletic Club
Payment Date   :   020691   Cheque Balance :   910.56
Cheque Number :   Cheque Amount :   910.56

Payment No.	Tp	Date	Inv.	Details	Amount	Discount	Tc
1	SI	310591	111	30 Nike Pegasus	910.56	0.00	T9
23	SI	100691	303	20 club vests	188.00	0.00	T1

Method of Payment : Automatic Manual

Either AUTOMATIC or MANUAL payment of the outstanding balances can be selected, the difference is that:

a) If the payment is a straightforward one select AUTOMATIC and watch the invoices being automatically paid off in sequence starting at the top.

b) If you only want to pay off certain invoices choose MANUAL and go through the invoices, selecting and pay-ing off only the ones required. This may be necessary if you want to keep track of which invoices have actually been paid and which are still outstanding.

For this example choose AUTOMATIC

When all the cheque has been used press the **ESC** key.

Again scrutinise your screen carefully for any mistakes.

Select **POST** if all is O.K. or **EDIT** to change your mind.

After entering the first set of details, enter the next set and so on (again choose AUTOMATIC).

When finished entering all the transactions, **ESC** back to the SALES LEDGER menu.

To look at the history of a specific account choose: TRAN-SACTION HISTORY

RETURN through the questions, this will display all the accounts in sequence.

Notes.
All unpaid invoices have an asterisk (*) beside the value.
Partly paid invoices have a (p) beside the value.
Paid invoices are unmarked.

ESC back to the MAIN menu.

That dealt with sales receipts. Now to do the same with purchase payments:

Select

PURCHASE LEDGER

Then

PAYMENTS

This follows the same steps as the sales ledger receipts. Enter these payments:

A/C	Date	Cheque no.	Nett Amnt
ASICS	160691	19000	1225.63
OAK	160691	19001	430.23
FAST	160691	19002	579.57
RON	160691	19004	734.12

Choose

AUTOMATIC then **ESC** and **POST**

for each transaction

The screen should look like this after the first payment has been entered

Financial Controller			Payments		30th June 1991	

N/C Bank 2   :   1200   N/C Bank Name : BANK CURRENT ACCOUNT
A/C Ref.   :   ASICS   A/C Name   : Olympian Sports UK Ltd
Payment Date :   160691   Cheque Balance : 0.00
Cheque Number : 19000   Cheque Amount : 1225.63

Payment	No.	Tp	Date	Inv.	Details	Amount	Discount	Tc
FULL	4	PI	310591	a3456	20 pairs shoes	0.00	0.00	T9
FULL	26	PI	020691	dd4563	20 prs asics shoes	0.00	0.00	T1

then **ESC** (twice) back to the MAIN menu.

It is worthwhile at this point looking at the daybook reports that can be generated from Sage, they list the transactions that you have entered in sequence and can provide useful information.

To do this select

SALES LEDGER then

DAY BOOKS and

SALES RECEIPTS

RETURN through the questions and then

ESC back and do the same for the PURCHASE LEDGER

Then **ESC** back to the MAIN menu.

Entering Direct Payments And Receipts.
These are items which appear on your Bank Statements and
examples of these include:

Bank Interest
Bank Charges
Mortgage Repayments
Rates Payments

Enter the information shown below

To do so choose:

NOMINAL LEDGER

then

BANK TRANSACTIONS

then

BANK PAYMENTS

Your screen will look like this after entering the data:

N/C	Dep.	Date	Cheque	Details	Nett Amnt	Tc	Tax Amnt
7103	0	010691	d/deb	rates to nov	556.14	T9	0.00
7901	0	010691	d/deb	bank charges to may	45.23	T9	0.00
7102	0	010691	d/deb	water rates to jun	56.34	T9	0.00
7303	0	010691	19005	car ins	345.54	T9	0.00
					1003.25		0.00

Financial Controller — Bank Payments — 30th June 1991
N/C Bank : BANK CURRENT ACCOUNT — Tax Rate : 0.000
N/C Name : — Batch Total : 1003.25

when finished

ESC and **POST**

then

ESC (twice)

to RETURN to the NOMINAL LEDGER menu.

> Note that all of these transactions use VAT code T9 (no VAT) because VAT is not charged on these transactions.

Cash payments and cash receipts are all dealt with in a similar way.

From the

NOMINAL LEDGER

choose

PETTY CASH TRANSACTIONS

then

CASH PAYMENTS

enter those transactions shown below

Financial Controller				Cash Payments			30th June 1991

N/C Name :

Tax Rate : 0.000
Batch Total : 12.44

N/C	Dep.	Date	Ref.	Details	Nett Amnt	Tc	Tax Amnt
5100	0	090691	hope	p&p on inv 301	1.96	T9	0.00
5100	0	090691	stamps	postage stamps	6.00	T9	0.00
5003	0	160691	food	coffee and milk	2.98	T9	0.00
5003	0	160691	photo	photostats	1.50	T9	0.00
					12.44		0.00

ESC and **POST** the transactions

then

ESC

back to the previous menu and choose

CASH RECEIPTS

Now enter the following:

Financial Controller				Cash Receipts			30th June 1991

N/C Name :

Tax Rate : 17.500
Batch Total : 217.95

N/C	Dep.	Date	Ref.	Details	Nett Amnt	Tc	Tax Amnt
4000	0	010691	cash	1 pr asics	39.14	T1	6.85
4001	0	020691	cash	1 pr nike	42.54	T1	7.45
4002	0	020691	cash	1 sunglasses	46.81	T1	8.19
4002	0	040691	cash	2 pr tracksters	20.41	T1	3.57
4000	0	090691	cash	1 pr NB shoes	29.79	T1	5.21
4002	0	090691	cash	1 watch	6.80	T1	1.19
					185.49		32.46

then **ESC** and **POST**

ESC (twice) back to the NOMINAL LEDGER menu.

To look at the Petty Cash account choose

CONTROL ACCOUNT HISTORY

then PETTY CASH

RETURN through the questions.

the display will look like this:

(note how it spreads over two pages on the screen)

| Financial Controller | | | Petty Cash | | | 30th June 1991 |

A/C Ref. : 1230   A/C Name : PETTY CASH

No.	Tp	Date	Ref	Details	Value	Debit	Credit
17	JD	310591		o/bal	7.98	7.98	
43	CP	090691	hope	p&p on inv 301	1.96		1.96
44	CP	090691	stamps	postage stamps	6.00		6.00
45	CP	160691	food	coffee and milk	2.98		2.98
46	CP	160691	photo	photostats	1.50		1.50
47	CR	010691	cash	1 pr asics	45.99	45.99	
48	CR	020691	cash	1 pr nike	49.99		
49	CR	020691	cash	1 sunglasses	55.00	104.99	
50	CR	040691	cash	2 pr tracksters	23.98	23.98	
51	CR	090691	cash	1 pr NB shoes	35.00		

Press ESC to finish, RETURN to continue

Financial Controller				Petty Cash		30th June 1991	

A/C Ref. : 1230   A/C Name : PETTY CASH

No.	Tp	Date	Ref	Details	Value	Debit	Credit
52	CR	090691	cash	1 watch	7.99	42.99	
					Totals :	225.93	12.44
					Balance :	213.49	

Press ESC to finish, RETURN to continue

When finished **ESC** (3 times) back to the MAIN menu.

END OF PERIOD ROUTINES (MONTHLY)

This should normally be carried out once a month, and needs to be done to produce VAT returns and in order to produce monthly accounts.

VAT Routine
As transactions are entered, any VAT content is posted to the relevant part of the Tax Control Account (2200). If this account has a Credit Balance then you owe the Customs & Excise. If the account has a Debit Balance then you are owed money by the Customs & Excise.

At the end of each accounting period (This may be a Week, Month, Quarter.), the balance from this account must be reduced to zero in order to make it easier to reconcile the VAT on the transactions for that period. This is done by transferring this amount to the VAT Liability Account (2201)

Carry out this procedure by:

Display the account for Tax Control (2200) by choosing:

NOMINAL LEDGER

followed by:

CONTROL ACCOUNT HISTORY

and

TAX CONTROL

RETURN through the questions, taking note of the balance (you may need to adjust the journal entry shown below by a penny, this is because of the way different processors round fractions.)

Then **ESC** back to the NOMINAL LEDGER menu and choose:

JOURNAL ENTRIES.

Enter the following:

Financial Controller				Journal Entries		30th June 1991

Date : 300691   Reference :
N/C Name : VAT LIABILITY   Batch Total :   0.00

N/C	Dep.	Details	Tc	Debit	Credit
2200	0	vat adj	T9		301.51
2201	0	vat adj	T9	301.51	

Batch Total MUST be ZERO before exit

This will make the Tax Control balance equal to zero.

ESC and **POST** the entry then

ESC back to the NOMINAL LEDGER menu.

We now need to create a journal entry to adjust for the closing stock.

select

JOURNAL ENTRIES

enter the following:

Financial Controller			Journal Entries			30th June 1991

Date   : 300691   Reference :
N/C Name : STOCK   Batch Total :   0.00

N/C	Dep.	Details	Tc	Debit	Credit
1001	0	o/stock b/s	T9		769.43
5200	0	o/stock p/l	T9	769.43	
5201	0	c/stock p/l	T9		3509.16
1001	0	c/stock b/s	T9	3509.16	

Batch Total MUST be ZERO before exit

ESC and **POST** the entries, and then **ESC** back to the NOMINAL LEDGER.

To print the Profit & Loss account and Balance sheet, from the

NOMINAL LEDGER menu

choose

MONTHLY ACCOUNTS

choose

P & L AND BALANCE SHEET

and follow through the questions, answering as necessary, but choosing P for Printer.

Your figures should be similar to those following, if they are not then print out an audit trail (a list of every transaction you have entered) and check carefully through it.

To obtain a printout of the audit trail select UTILITIES (from the main menu) and then select AUDIT TRAIL

	This Month		Year To Date	
Sales				
PRODUCT SALES	1775.49		1775.49	
		1775.49		1775.49
Purchases				
PURCHASES	3502.69		3502.69	
PURCHASE CHARGES	7.69		7.69	
STOCK	(2739.73)		(2739.73)	
		770.92		770.92
Gross Profit		1004.57		1004.57
Overheads				
RENT & RATES	612.48		612.48	
MOTOR EXPENSES	345.54		345.54	
BANK CHARGES	45.23		45.23	
		1003.25		1003.25
Nett Profit		1.32		1.32

	This Month		Year To Date	
Fixed Assets				
OFFICE EQUIPMENT		2400.00		2400.00
FURNITURE & FIXTURES		1200.00		1200.00
		3600.00		3600.00
Current Assets				
STOCK	3509.16		3509.16	
DEBTORS	1304.25		1304.25	
DEPOSITS/CASH	213.49		213.49	
VAT LIABILITY	301.51		301.51	
	5328.41		5328.41	
Current Liabilities				
CREDITORS	3105.79		3105.79	
BANK ACCOUNT	1655.69		1655.69	
	4761.48		4761.48	
Net Current Assets		566.93		566.93
Net Assets		4166.93		4166.93
Financed by				
RESERVES	4165.61		4165.61	
Profit/Loss Accoun	1.32		1.32	
		4166.93		4166.93

ESC back to the main menu and you have finished the first month's accounting records.

SETTING UP THE DATAFILES
READY FOR THE NEXT MONTH

From the NOMINAL LEDGER menu choose:

MONTHLY ACCOUNTS

followed by

CREATE END OF MONTH ACCOUNTS

this allows the creation of separate files for each month and when you produce profit & loss accounts and balance sheets, you can show the individual months' figures as well as the cumulative year to date figures.

This *must* only be carried out after printing the monthly accounts *and* backing up the month's files onto a floppy disc (remember to label the floppy disc and to keep it in a safe place in case it is ever needed. Remember to have at least one floppy disc copy of *each* month's figures)

DEALING WITH THE NEXT MONTH'S TRANSACTIONS

Set the system date to 300791

Having successfully completed the first month's accounting entries, you can now begin to enter the second month's.

If you forget how to carry out a specific activity, simply look back at the previous section.

Sales Ledger
Fast Feet have gained some new customers and you must enter their names and other details into the Sales Ledger before you can enter the sales you have made to them. The new accounts are:

ANG   The Angels Running Club
                6 The Borrows
                West Chinnock
                Yeovil, Somerset
                BA45 7SA

JOGG   The Jolly Joggers
                45 High Street
                Street
                Somerset
                ST6 8TR

RAP   The Rapid Running Club
                c/o The Sports Shop
                West Street
                Chippenham, Wilts
                CH7 3DC

Now you can enter all the invoices you have sent out in the second month (to both the new and old customers):

A/C	Date	Inv.	N/C	Dep.	Details	Nett Amnt	Tc	Tax Amnt
RAP	030791	305	4001	0	8 club vests	61.28	T1	10.72
ABLE	030791	306	4001	0	3 prs sunglasses	153.19	T1	26.81
ABLE	030791	306	4000	0	1 pr asics shoes	38.29	T1	6.70
JOGG	050791	307	4002	0	3 stopwatches	20.43	T1	3.57
TROT	070791	308	4002	0	5 bumbags	34.04	T1	5.96
TROT	070791	308	4000	0	2 pr nike shoes	59.57	T1	10.43
HOPE	110791	309	4000	0	4 prs NB shoes	153.19	T1	26.81
SLOW	150791	310	4001	0	20 prs tracksters	102.13	T1	17.87
ANG	210791	311	4001	0	5 vests	38.30	T1	6.70
ANG	210791	311	4001	0	5 prs tracksters	25.53	T1	4.47
						685.95		120.04

Fast Feet have received the following money from their customers during the month.

A/C	Date	Nett Am'nt
SLOW	020791	235.00
TROT	050791	352.50
SLOW	090791	528.75
ABLE	100791	412.99
JOGG	150791	24.00

Pay these AUTOMATICally.

Purchase Ledger
Having dealt with the SALES LEDGER, you can enter transactions into the PURCHASE LEDGER.

> note: the order of dealing with the different ledgers is simply one of convenience for working with this example, they can be dealt with in any order

The firm have received invoices from the following suppliers during the second month.

A/C	Date	Inv.	N/C	Dep.	Details	Nett Amnt	Tc	Tax Amnt
RON	020791	8923	5001	0	25 prs tracksters	148.94	T1	26.06
SWE	020791	ff570	5000	0	20 prs nike shoes	425.53	T1	74.47
FAST	100791	s390	5002	0	10 prs bumbags	46.81	T1	8.19
FAST	110791	s391	5002	0	4 prs watches	22.00	T1	3.85
						643.28		112.57

Fast Feet have made payments to the following suppliers during the month.

A/C	Date	Cheque no.	Nett Am'nt
SWE	020791	19006	910.63
OAK	060791	19007	1997.88
SWE	080791	19008	144.40
FAST	100791	19009	52.88
RON	150791	19010	175.00

Pay these AUTOMATICally

Cash Transactions

Remember that Cash transactions are dealt with through the NOMINAL LEDGER (then selecting PETTY CASH TRANSACTIONS).

The following cash was received:

N/C	Dep.	Date	Ref.	Details	Nett Amnt	Tc	Tax Amnt
4000	0	020791	cash	1 pr nike shoes	42.54	T1	7.45
4001	0	020791	cash	1 club vest	6.81	T1	1.19
4002	0	050791	cash	1 stopwatch	6.38	T1	1.12
4000	0	050791	cash	1 pr asics	42.54	T1	7.45
4001	0	100791	cash	2 pr sunglasses	110.64	T1	19.36
4002	0	110791	cash	1 bumbag	6.38	T1	1.12
4000	0	130791	cash	1 pr NB	46.80	T1	8.19
4001	0	130791	cash	2 pr tracksters	20.43	T1	3.57
4000	0	150791	cash	1 pr nike shoes	34.03	T1	5.96
4000	0	190791	cash	1 pr asics	76.59	T1	13.40
4000	0	190791	cash	2 pr asics	170.20	T1	29.78
					563.34		98.59

and the cash payments below were made during the month:

N/C	Dep.	Date	Ref.	Details	Nett Amnt	Tc	Tax Amnt
5003	0	020791	food	milk & coffee	9.87	T9	0.00
5100	0	070791	post	stamps	2.00	T9	0.00
5003	0	100791	food	meal for customer	13.87	T9	0.00
					25.74		0.00

Bank Payments

N/C	Dep.	Date	Cheque	Details	Nett Amnt	Tc	Tax Amnt
7901	0	300791	d/deb	bank charges jun	89.23	T9	0.00
7301	0	300791	19011	car service	168.51	T1	29.49
7302	0	300791	19012	road tax	100.00	T9	0.00
					357.74		29.49

So far in the second month's transactions you have used parts of the program already covered in the first month's work. These types of transactions are the main stay of most accounting systems and it is important that you (and your staff) are familiar with them.

There are many other facilities available within Sage, and we are now going to look at those you are more likely to need, starting with the processing of refunds.

PROCESSING REFUNDS

It is often the situation in business that refunds have to be made to a customer. Fast Feet have had 15 pairs of socks returned by The Trotters club.

To process the refund select the

SALES LEDGER then

REFUNDS

and finally REFUND INVOICE

Enter the account reference

(in this case TROT)

and a list of the fully paid invoices for that customer will be displayed.

Move the cursor onto the correct invoice you wish to refund and press **RETURN**. (the invoice is the first one in the list).

The invoice will be marked as "REFUNDED" (to cancel a refund press **RETURN** when the cursor in over a refunded invoice)

ESC and **POST** the transaction and the necessary adjustments to the bank account, etc., are made

ESC back to the SALES LEDGER and select

DAYBOOKS and then

SALES INVOICES

and **RETURN** through the questions.

You will be able to see the refund showing up as the last entry

ESC back to the NOMINAL LEDGER and choose

CONTROL ACCOUNT HISTORY followed by

BANK ACCOUNTS

and **RETURN** through the questions

the last entry will show the refund.

You will have to actually write the cheque using the information shown in the Bank Account.

Although you have only dealt with processing refunds to customers, refunds from suppliers work in exactly the same way.

---

note: Sage can only refund complete invoices, they cannot be partially refunded

---

DEALING WITH ERRORS

The *first* rule is *always* check your entries before posting.

However mistakes or errors will happen, and if they do there are several possible courses of action.

When you realise you have made an error, do not blindly try to correct it but follow through this sequence of activities:

Print out all the affected accounts and find out where the mistake occurred.
From these printouts decide on the necessary adjustments and write them down on paper.
Then, still using the printouts, make the adjustments you have just written down to the relevant accounts to make sure that they have the required result.
Only then enter the adjustments onto the computer files.
There is nothing more likely to cause utter chaos and confusion than to make entries onto the computer files without care and thought.

Here are a couple of ways of adjusting for mistakes (there are others such as journal entries)

Posting Error Corrections
It is common for an error to be made to a posting as a result of mistyping or misreading or just plain carelessness. As suggested it is always best to thoroughly check the entries *before* posting them as adjusting for errors is tedious.

To alter an incorrect posting it is first necessary to know the transaction number (which can be obtained by selecting UTILITIES from the MAIN menu and then selecting AUDIT TRAIL)

There are two types of error correction, firstly a reverse posting which cancels the original, and secondly an adjustment to the original posting. We will look at each of these in turn.

Reverse Posting

Select UTILITIES (from the MAIN menu) then

DATA FILE UTILITIES then

POSTING ERROR CORRECTION

and REVERSE POSTING

The item we are going to reverse (cancel) is item 77 on the AUDIT TRAIL, a purchase invoice from FASTRACK of LEEDS (check the audit trail to make sure youhave picked the right transaction)

Enter the item number on the form and the screen should look like this

---

Financial Controller	Reverse Posting	30th July 1991

Transaction Number : 77

Purchase Invoice : Corrective Posting

   Purchase Credit Note to A/C "FAST " and N/C "5002 " for 22.00 net, and 3.85 tax.

   This Credit Note will be fully allocated against the original Invoice.

   Proceed with Correction? : No Yes

Answer **Y** for YES and **ESC** back to the MAIN menu.

As we proceed the correction will be carried out and although the original invoice will still show, its effect will have been cancelled out, and as far as you are concerned it will not have existed.

There will however be a balance on the suspense account which needs to be journalised by

Debiting a/c 4001	25.69	
Crediting a/c 9998		25.69

Carry out this journal entry (use tax code T9)

You can see the effect of the correction by selecting the

PURCHASE LEDGER and then

DAY BOOKS and

PURCHASE CREDIT NOTES.

RETURN through the questions

It is also worth looking at this stage at the history of the account for FASTRACK. To do this select

PURCHASE LEDGER again, followed by

TRANSACTION HISTORY.

Enter FAST as the reference and **RETURN** through the rest of the questions, the screen will look like this

Financial Controller				Transaction History			30th July 1991
A/C Ref. : FAST					A/C Name : Fastrack		
No.	Tp	Date	Ref	Details	Value	Debit	Credit
6	PI	310591	f7f8	50 club vests	250.56		250.56
28	PI	070691	s234	10 prs watches	64.63		64.63
29	PI	090691	s235	50 club vests	264.38		264.38
31	PI	160691	s345	10 bumbags	52.88		52.88
37	PP	160691	19002	Purchase Payment	579.57	579.57	
76	PI	100791	s390	10 prs bumbags	55.00*		55.00
77	PI	110791	s391	4 prs watches	25.85		25.85
81	PP	100791	19009	Purchase Payment	52.88	52.88	
104	PC	230691	ERROR	Reverse No. 77	25.85	25.85	

Amount Outstanding :	55.00	Credit Limit :	0.00
Amount paid this period :	632.45	Turnover YTD :	622.37

Press ESC to finish, RETURN to continue

ESC back to the MAIN menu.

Correct Posting

Here you are not cancelling a transaction but merely altering it, perhaps because of a mistyping.

Select UTILITIES (from the MAIN menu)

then DATA FILE UTILITIES

then POSTING ERROR CORRECTION

and CORRECT POSTING

Enter the transaction number, this time you want to alter item 75

Alter the details to

```
20 prs nike air sh.
```

The screen should look like this:

Financial Controller		Correct Posting		30th July 1991

Transaction Number	:	75
Type	:	PI
Sales/Purchase A/C Code	:	SWE
Nominal A/C Code	:	5000
Department Code	:	O
Transaction Date	:	020791
Invoice Reference	:	ff570
Details	:	20 prs nike air sh.
Nett Amount	:	425.53
Tax Amount	:	74.47
Tax Code	:	T1
Payment Date	:	
Cheque Reference	:	
Amount Paid	:	0.00
Fully Paid Flag	:	N
Next transaction for A/C	:	78
Next transaction for N/C	:	0

and then **RETURN**, then **ESC** and enter **Y** to process the entry and **ESC** back to the MAIN menu.

To check the alteration, select the PURCHASES LEDGER and then TRANSACTION HISTORY and enter SWE as the reference, **RETURN**ing through the other questions.

PRODUCING THE ACCOUNTS FOR MONTH 2

At the end of the second month, you will produce monthly accounts in the same way as the first month.

The following text is a summary of the tasks that have to be carried out to do this, if you are unsure *why* you are doing a task, look back to the explanation at the end of the first month's figures.

End Of Period Routines (Monthly)

VAT routine.
Display the account for Tax Control (2200) by choosing:

NOMINAL LEDGER followed by

CONTROL ACCOUNT HISTORY and

TAX CONTROL

RETURN through the questions, taking a note of the balance (again there may be a penny difference from that shown below)

Then **ESC** back to the NOMINAL LEDGER menu and choose: JOURNAL ENTRIES.

Remember that the date can be entered by using **F5** and the previous line can be copied by using **F6**.

Enter the following:

Financial Controller		Journal Entries			30th July 1991

Date : 300791 | | | | Reference : tax ad

N/C Name : | | | | Batch Total : | 0.00

N/C	Dep.	Details	Tc	Debit	Credit
2200	0	vat adj month 2	T9	80.42	
2201	0	vat adj month 2	T9		80.42

Batch Total MUST be ZERO before exit

This will make the Tax Control balance equal to zero.

ESC and **POST** the journal.

Now create a journal entry to adjust for the closing stock, so **ESC** back to the NOMINAL LEDGER menu and select:

JOURNAL ENTRIES

enter the following:

Financial Controller		Journal Entries			30th July 1991

Date : 300791 | | | | Reference : month2

N/C Name : | | | | Batch Total : | 0.00

N/C	Dep.	Details	Tc	Debit	Credit
1001	0	o/stock b/s	T9		3509.16
5200	0	o/stock p/l	T9	3509.16	
5201	0	c/stock p/l	T9		3381.52
1001	0	c/stock b/s	T9	3381.52	

Batch Total MUST be ZERO before exit

ESC and **POST** the entries, and then **ESC** back to the NOMINAL LEDGER.

At this point it is worthwhile printing out a Trial Balance showing the balance on each Nominal Ledger account. You can then compare the balances with the figures appearing in the Profit and Loss Account and the Balance Sheet (for the year to date).

The Trial Balance at the end of the second month should look like this:

Ref.	Accounts Name	Debit	Credit
0030	OFFICE EQUIPMENT	2400.00	
0040	FURNITURE AND FIXTURES	1200.00	
1001	STOCK	3381.52	
1100	DEBTORS CONTROL ACCOUNT	557.00	
1200	BANK CURRENT ACCOUNT		3796.16
1230	PETTY CASH	849.68	
2100	CREDITORS CONTROL ACCOUNT		555.00
2201	VAT LIABILITY	221.09	
3100	RESERVES		4165.61
4000	shoe sales	1782.68	
4001	clothing sales		1075.16
4002	equipment sales		141.25
5000	shoe purchases	1898.42	
5001	clothing purchases	2074.26	
5002	equipment purchases	146.81	
5003	miscellaneous purchases	28.22	
5100	CARRIAGE	9.96	
5200	OPENING STOCK	4278.59	
5201	CLOSING STOCK		6890.68
7102	WATER RATES	56.34	
7103	GENERAL RATES	556.14	
7301	REPAIRS AND SERVICING	168.51	
7302	LICENCES	100.00	
7303	VEHICLE INSURANCE	345.54	
7901	BANK CHARGES	134.46	
		18406.54	18406.54

To print the Profit & Loss account and Balance sheet, select the

NOMINAL LEDGER menu

then choose

MONTHLY ACCOUNTS and P & L AND BALANCE SHEET

and follow through the questions, answering as necessary, but choosing **P** for Printer.

Your figures should be similar to those below. If they are not, then print out an audit trail (a list of every transaction you have entered) and check carefully through it.

To obtain a printout of the audit trail select UTILITIES (from the main menu) and then select AUDIT TRAIL

FAST FEET	Management Reports — Profit & Loss Account			Date : 300791
				Page : 1
	This Month		Year To Date	
Sales				
PRODUCT SALES	1223.60		2999.09	
		1223.60		2999.09
Purchases				
PURCHASES	645.02		4147.71	
PURCHASE CHARGES	2.00		9.96	
STOCK	127.64		(2612.09)	
		774.66		1545.58
Gross Profit		448.94		1453.51
Overheads				
RENT & RATES			612.48	
MOTOR EXPENSES	268.51		614.05	
BANK CHARGES	89.23		134.46	
		357.74		1360.99
Nett Profit		91.20		92.52

```
FAST FEET          Management Reports — Balance Sheet          Date : 300791
                      This Month                                Year To Date

Fixed Assets

OFFICE EQUIPMENT                                                2400.00
FURNITURE & FIXTURES                                            1200.00
                                       0.00                     3600.00

Current Assets

STOCK                      (127.64)                    3381.52
DEBTORS                    (747.25)                     557.00
DEPOSITS/CASH               636.19                      849.68
VAT LIABILITY                                           221.09
                           (238.70)                    5009.29

Current Liabilities

CREDITORS                 (2550.79)                     555.00
BANK ACCOUNT               2140.47                     3796.16
VAT LIABILITY                80.42
                           (329.90)                    4351.16

Net Current Assets                     91.20                     658.13

Net Assets                             91.20                    4258.13

Financed by

RESERVES                                               4165.61
Profit/Loss                 91.20                        92.52
                                       91.20                    4258.13
```

ESC back to the MAIN menu and you have finished the first month's accounting records.

When reading the printed accounts note that the year to date figures reflect the cumulative situation; the figures for This Month only reflect what has actually happened during that month

Remember to set up the datafiles ready for the next month by selecting

MONTHLY ACCOUNTS

followed by

CREATE END OF MONTH ACCOUNTS

This *must* only be carried out after printing the monthly accounts and backing up that month's files onto a floppy disc (remember to label the floppy disc and to keep it in a safe place in case it is ever needed. Remember to have at least one floppy disc copy of *each* months figures)

REPORTS

After having entered transactions for two months, you can now look at the Transaction History reports that can be produced. These display the entries that have been made in the relevant ledgers.

Choose SALES LEDGER from the MAIN menu and then

TRANSACTION HISTORY

RETURN through the question and there will be displayed on the screen all the transactions that have taken place on each of the Sales Accounts.

If you did not want to see all the accounts or you only wanted to see the details for a specific period, then instead of RETURNing through the questions, type in the relevant answers.

ESC back to the MAIN menu and

Then PURCHASE LEDGER and

TRANSACTION HISTORY

Look through the data displayed and then do the same thing for the NOMINAL LEDGER.

Report Generator
Sage also has a Report Generator which can be used with any of the following:

Sales ledger   Purchase ledger
Nominal ledger   Management reports
Sales order processing   Stock control
Purchase order processing

To Use A Report
From the main menu choose REPORT GENERATOR, then

SALES LEDGER

The following screen will be displayed:

Financial Controller	Sales Ledger	30th July 1991

NAME	TITLE
AGED	Sales Ledger Aged Debtors Analysis
AGED	Sales Ledger Aged Debtors Analysis
DEBT	Sales Accounts 30 Day Debt exceeding 1000 pounds
DEPT	Sales Ledger Departmental Analysis
LEDG	Sales Ledger Comma Separated Value File
LIMIT	Sales Accounts Credit Limit Exceeded
SELL	Top Customer List
TURN	Sales Ledger Nett Turnover Month & Year to date

To Run A Report
Make sure the cursor highlights the report name AGED and
press **RETURN**.

The following question will be displayed:

Do you want to : Run Edit Print Delete

Choose **RUN** and **RETURN** through the questions, a copy of
the report will then be printed out.

The report will look similar to this:

```
FAST FEET              Sales Ledger Aged Debtors Analysis          Date : 300791

                                                                      Page : 1

A/C   Account Name         Turnover Balance Current 30 Day 60 Day 90 Day Older
ANG   The Angels Running Club  63.83   75.00  75.00   0.00   0.00   0.00  0.00
HOPE  The Hopeful Hobblers    681.51  180.00 180.00   0.00   0.00   0.00  0.00
JOGG  The Slow Joggers         20.43    0.00   0.00   0.00   0.00   0.00  0.00
RAP   The Rapid Running Club   61.28   72.00  72.00   0.00   0.00   0.00  0.00
SLOW  The Slow Joggers        752.13  120.00 120.00   0.00   0.00   0.00  0.00
TROT  The Trotters            393.61  110.00 110.00   0.00   0.00   0.00  0.00

                            1972.79  557.00 557.00   0.00   0.00   0.00  0.00
```

Now move the cursor onto the report for TURN and select this by **RETURN**ing:

The report will look like this:

```
FAST FEET                              Sales Ledger Nett Turnover Month
& Year to date                         Date : 300791

Page : 1

                                       Turnover          Turnover
A/C         Account Name                    YTD               MTH

ABLE        The Able Athletic Club      1262.04           1262.04
ANG         The Angels Running Club       63.83             63.83
HOPE        The Hopeful Hobblers         681.51            681.51
JOGG        The Jolly Joggers             20.43             20.43
RAP         The Rapid Running Club        61.28             61.28
SLOW        The Slow Joggers             752.13            752.13
TROT        The Trotters                 393.61            419.30

                                        3234.83           3260.52
```

This section has given an idea of the various reports that can be automatically generated by Sage (it is also possible to produce customised reports).

STOCK CONTROL

Reset the system date to 310891

The stock control module can be used as a stand-alone unit or it can be integrated with the ledgers. For example if the option to invoice from stock is used, then the invoices can be produced and the sales ledger updated without any other entries being made.

Due to the success of the computerised ledger accounting, Fast Feet have decided to computerise their stock control from the start of month 3.

Setting Up The Stock Categories
To begin to use the stock control it is necessary first to set up the stock categories (this means entering the types of stock that will be held).

From the MAIN menu

choose

STOCK CONTROL then

choose

CATEGORIES

The screen looks like this (after entering the data)

Financial Controller			Categories	31st August 1991
Category	Name	1	: SHOES	
..	..	2	: CLOTHING	
..	..	3	: EQUIPMENT	
..	..	4	: MISCELLANEOUS	
..	..	5	:	
..	..	6	:	
..	..	7	:	
..	..	8	:	
..	..	9	:	
..	..	10	:	
..	..	11	:	
..	..	12	:	
..	..	13	:	
..	..	14	:	
..	..	15	:	

Complete the list for the categories as shown above.

ESC back to the STOCK CONTROL menu.

Note: The program can cope with up to 90 categories of stock

Entering Stock Items
Details of the various stock items can now be entered (not the actual quantities which come later, but the actual items of stock themselves)

From the STOCK CONTROL menu

choose

UPDATE STOCK DETAILS

Enter the stock details shown below

(after completing each entry **ESC** and **POST**)

SCde	Desc	Cat	name	Sale pr.	Unit	R/L.	R/	Qnt.	Nom. code	Supp
001	Nike	1	Shoes	42.55	Pair		10	5	5000	SWE
002	New Balance	1	Shoes	51.05	Pair		10	10	5000	SWE
003	ASICS Gellyte3	1	Shoes	59.56	Pair		10	5	5000	ASICS
004	ASICS GT3	1	Shoes	76.59	Pair		5	3	5000	ASICS
005	Vests	2	Clothing	7.65	Each		15	10	5001	FAST
006	Tracksters	2	Clothing	11.06	Pair		20	10	5001	RON
007	Sunglasses	2	Clothing	53.61	Pair		5	5	5001	OAK
008	Bumbags	3	Equipment	6.38	Each		10	10	5002	FAST
009	Watches	3	Equipment	5.78	Each		10	5	5002	FAST

The sale prices should be entered net of VAT (as VAT is automatically added when an invoice is created).

ESC back to the STOCK CONTROL menu when these have all been entered and select

STOCK DETAILS (**RETURN** through the questions)

This displays a list of all the stock items (code by code).

Opening Stock
Opening stock must be entered in order to keep track of all stock movement.

Choose

STOCK CONTROL then

ADJUSTMENTS IN

Enter the following:

S/code	Description	Qnt	Cost	Date
001	Nike	20	24.58	300791
002	New Balance	9	31.00	300791
003	Asics gellyte3	5	24.20	300791
004	Asics GT3	4	35.00	300791
005	Vests	14	5.50	300791
006	Tracksters	116	6.12	300791
007	Sunglasses	34	42.50	300791
008	Bumbags	14	4.50	300791
009	Watches	10	5.50	300791

The screen will now look like this after entering the first item:

Financial Controller	Adjustments In		31st August 1991
Stock Code	: 001		
Description	: NIKE		
Quantity	: 20.00	Qty in Stock	: 0.00
		Qty Allocated	: 0.00
Cost Price	: 24.58	Qty On-Order	: 0.00
Sale Price	: 42.55		
Narrative	: Opening Stock		
Reference	:	Last Sale	:
Date	: 300791	Last Purchase	:

ESC and **POST** each transaction

When finished **ESC** back to the STOCK CONTROL menu.

Look at the Stock Valuation Report

To do so choose:

STOCK VALUATION then

RETURN through the questions.

> Note that the total stock figure is the same as that used for the closing stock figure for the second month (July).

Invoicing From Stock
Sage enables you to create invoices from the stock records, which automatically update both the stock records and the ledger accounts at the same time (thus saving considerable effort and possible mistakes)

From the MAIN menu

Choose

SALES LEDGER then

INVOICE PRODUCTION then

INVOICING FROM STOCK

Entering Details Of Stock Sold

> Invoice numbers will automatically be incremented by one as each new invoice is entered.
> The invoice number may be changed to the one you wish to start from using the cursor
> keys to move up, and then typing in the required number.

Alter the date to 010891 and press **RETURN**.

Enter ABLE as the sales reference for the first customer.

The name and address will be automatically shown on the screen

> The cursor will now move to the delivery address area. As this is the same as the invoice
> address then just press the down arrow key to pass over it, if nothing is to be entered
> in a field — press the down arrow key

The customer Order Number is the reference on the order from your customer

Enter AB76 and **RETURN**.

Enter Stock code as 002

Enter quantity as 2

Then **ESC** back to the first screen

The first screen will look like this after entering the details:

Financial Controller	Invoicing from Stock	31st August 1991

```
Invoice No.          :  1

Date                 :  010891
Sales Ref.           :  ABLE

Customer Name        :  The Able Athletic Club  Order No.           :           0
Customer Address     :  The Council Track       Customer Order No.  :      ab76
       ..            :  Yeovil
       ..            :  Somerset
       ..            :  BA21 6RD

Telephone            :

                                                Total Nett          :      102.10
Delivery Name        :  --- AS INVOICED---      Total Tax           :       17.87
                                                Delivery Address    :
       ..            :                          Total Gross         :      119.97
       ..            :
       ..            :                          Early Payment       :      119.97
```

The display at the bottom right will show the money details for this item
The display at the top right is the rolling total for all the items on the invoice.

then **ESC** and **SAVE** the invoice.

Having entered the first invoice, create the following invoices, entering the details shown below:

Date	Sales Ref	Customer O/N	Stock Code	Quantity
010891	TROT	TR99	008	4
010891	RAP	RA34	004	1
010891	HOPE	HO11	006	16

If you need to enter more than one item onto an invoice, use the cursor keys to move onto a new page and enter the additional data (instead of **ESC**aping back to the original screen)

Fast Feet are going to invoice three items to *The Slow Joggers*.

Date	Sales Ref	Customer O/N	Stock Code	Quantity
010891	SLOW	SL5	009	2
			007	1
			005	10

When finished **ESC** back to the

INVOICE PRODUCTION menu and choose

DISPLAY INDEX.

RETURN through the questions.

This will list all invoices, giving details as to whether they have been printed and / or posted to the ledgers.

Printing Invoices

RETURN to the INVOICE PRODUCTION screen and choose:

PRINT INVOICES

RETURN through the questions.

This will print the invoices ready for delivery to your customers (headed notepaper can be used)

Posting Invoices To The Sales Ledger

To post the invoice details to the ledgers:

Choose UPDATE LEDGERS

Press **RETURN** and all posting of invoices to the ledger accounts will be done automatically. **RETURN** through the questions and a report will be printed out.

Now **ESC** back to the SALES LEDGER menu and choose:

TRANSACTION HISTORY

RETURN through the questions and the stock transactions that have been invoiced will be shown, account by account. Check these against the report you have just printed out.

Remember the * items mean an unpaid invoice

Looking at what has happened

To look at the various other reports that can be usefully produced at this point **ESC** back to the MAIN menu and choose

STOCK CONTROL then STOCK VALUATION

RETURN through the questions and this will produce a listing of the stock value at the date in question

finally choose

PROFIT REPORT followed by

YEAR TO DATE

RETURN through the questions and this produces an item by item listing of the profit produced (selling price less cost price)

Purchasing New Stock

Fast Feet have purchased new stock and you have to enter this into both the purchase ledger and the stock records.

Starting with the purchase ledger:

From the MAIN menu select

PURCHASE LEDGER then

BATCHED DATA ENTRY then

PURCHASE INVOICES

Enter the following data from your suppliers' invoices:

| A/C Name : | | | | | Tax Rate : | | 17.500 |
| N/C Name : | | | | | Batch Total : | | 218.00 |

A/C	Date	Inv.	N/C	Dep. Details	Nett Amnt	Tc	Tax Amnt
FAST	100891	s456	5001	0 10 vests	46.81	T1	8.19
SWE	100891	ff623	5000	0 3 NB shoes	79.15	T1	13.85
ASICS	100891	dd7896	5000	0 2 prs GT3	59.57	T1	10.43
					185.53		32.47

ESC and **POST** then **ESC** back to the PURCHASE LEDGER menu and select

DAYBOOKS and

PURCHASE INVOICES

to check that the entries have been made.

Now to enter the transactions into the STOCK records select

MAIN menu then

choose

STOCK CONTROL then

ADJUSTMENTS IN

and enter the following data (which comes from the invoices entered above)

Code	Quantity	Narrative	Date
005	10	Invoice	100891
002	3	Invoice	100891
004	2	Invoice	100891

Check the stock valuation and stock history reports to ensure that the entries have been made

Now to finish off Month 3 produce the following reports:

Trial Balance

Profit and Loss Account

Balance Sheet

Remember to put through journal entries for STOCK and TAX (pick up the stock figure from the stock records and the tax figure from the control account). Also remember to create END OF MONTH ACCOUNTS.

Compare the figures with last month's accounts to see how the firm has progressed.

USING THE TEXT EDITOR TO CREATE LETTERS

Sage has a text editor built-in, which while not as sophisticated as a specialist word-processing program does enable you to send customised letters to your customers and suppliers.

The text editor can be used in several ways from within the Sage program, one of which is to send reminders to customers.

Fast Feet want to write to all their customers who owe them money, to chase them for payment.

To do this from the MAIN menu select UTILITIES then

STATIONERY LAYOUTS

At this point the screen looks like this

Sage Menu Program	STATIONERY Layouts	31st August 1991

Accounts Letters
Invoices (Stock)
Invoices (Free Text)
Sales Orders
Purchase Orders
Payslips
Payroll Giros
Payroll Cheques

Then select ACCOUNTS LETTERS

RETURN on the filename and the screen will look like this (the letter spreads over 2 pages, use PGUP and PGDN and the cursor keys to move around the letter)

Filename : OVERDUE.LET   Line :   1 Column :   1 [I]   Memory (K):   341

      Account Name   Date #3
      Address Line #1
      Address Line #2
      Address Line #3
      Address Line #4

Dear Sirs,

                    OVERDUE ACCOUNT $ Balance

Filename : OVERDUE.LET   Line :   44 Column :   1 [I]   Memory (K):   341

      With Reference to the above balance which is still outstanding
      on your account. May I remind you that our terms are strictly 30
      days nett and $ 60 Day   is more than 60 days overdue.

        Your remittance by RETURN would be appreciated.

                    Yours faithfully,
                    SAGESOFT LTD.,

                    Paul Walker,
                    COMPANY ACCOUNTANT.

Move the cursor to the following

```
$ 60 DAY
```

and delete the words 60 DAY but not the $ sign.

Press **F4** and move the cursor onto the word

```
CURRENT
```

and press **RETURN**.

This should position the word CURRENT where 60 DAY was.

ESC and **SAVE** the file.

ESC back to the MAIN menu and select

SALES LEDGER then

LETTERS

and **RETURN** through the question *except* entering

0	for No of days outstanding
310891	for the date

Look at the letters printed out (Customised STATIONERY can be used when you get the operation working live)

BACKING UP (AND RESTORING YOUR DATA)

After each session at the keyboard entering data it is a wise precaution against either fire, damage or hardware theft to take backups of all data files. This is done just after finishing the sessions by choosing:

UTILITIES

from the MAIN menu

and then choosing

BACKUP UTILITIES

Place a blank disc in drive A:

then select

BACKUP DATA FILES

and

ACCOUNTS DATA FILES

answer Y for YES to the question and the screen will show all the file names as they are copied.

This is a safety net. The floppy disc should be transferred to separate premises in case of fire or theft. Providing you have this copy you will still be in business. It may also be useful if, after starting up next day, you make such a mess of entering the new data that it is easier to restore the old data and start again.

Murphy's Law states that if you keep at least two copies of all your data files you will probably never need to use them (on the other hand !)

If it is necessary to RESTORE the data select

UTILITIES then

BACKUP UTILITIES then

RESTORE DATA FILES and

ACCOUNTS DATA FILES

YEAR END ROUTINES AND MAKING ROOM ON YOUR DISC

Depending on how many transactions are made by your firm, at some time or other you will need to delete the old invoices which have been paid, etc., and only bring forward the current live transactions.

If this is not done then eventually you will run out of disc space. This routine must be carried out at the accounting year end in order to clear the ledgers for the next year's transactions.

To do this choose :

UTILITIES then

DATA FILE UTILITIES then

DATA FILE CHANGES then

RECONFIGURATION

What actually happens is that the completed transactions are deleted and the unfinished ones brought forward to begin the next period.

ESC back to the UTILITIES menu and select:

YEAR END and

ACCOUNTS and

RETURN through the questions.

ESC back to the UTILITIES menu again and select

DATA FILE UTILITIES then

DATA FILE CHANGES then

RECONFIGURATION

this removes the journal entries created by the Accounts Year End procedure.

You may also need to do the Year End Procedure with the Stock records if you have computerised them.

GETTING STARTED (WITH COMPUTERISING YOUR ACCOUNTS)

Before you can begin to enter any actual transactions, you must enter details of your customers, suppliers and nominal accounts (types of Sales categories, Purchase categories, Overheads and expenses)

Remember that:

Sales Ledger —   contains all information on transactions with your customers e.g. Invoices, discounts allowed and payments made.

Purchase ledger —   contains all information on transactions with your suppliers.

Nominal ledger —   contains all information relating to a certain product or service e.g. Sales, Petrol, Insurance, Purchases, etc. It also contains accounts such as Bank account, Petty cash, Assets (Cars, furniture), etc.

When computerising stock records, write down the categories or types of stock you need.

WHAT TO DO BEFORE SETTING UP COMPUTERISED ACCOUNTS

1. List all invoices for sales made by you but not paid for by your customer (*Debtors*). Also list outstanding credit notes issued to your customers.

2. List all purchases made by you but not yet paid for (*Creditors*). Also make note of any outstanding credit notes you have received from your suppliers.

3. Write down:

   Bank Balances (taking into account cheques paid but not yet presented).

   Total cash on hand.

   Outstanding VAT

4. By looking back over last year's transactions calculate:

   The number of different sales accounts.

   The number of different purchase or expense accounts.

   The number of nominal accounts needed.

RESIZING FILES

Before doing this, please take backups of your data.

This routine is used

1. On initial set-up.

2. When you want to erase all the data.

3. When you want to increase the number of accounts within the ledgers (for example you may have not taken account of the rapid increase in your business and you need to create more sales ledger accounts).

From the MAIN menu choose

UTILITIES then

choose

DATA FILE UTILITIES then

DATA FILE CHANGES

followed by

RESIZE DATA FILES

answer N when asked if there is any existing data (assuming you do not want to carry forward the existing data)

and Y when asked if the default nominal codes are wanted (if they are)

When finished, **ESC** back to the MAIN menu.

VERSIONS OF THE SAGE PROGRAM

The several programs that make up the different versions of Sage are as follows:

1. **Sage Bookkeeper**
   This is the simplest version and consists of an integrated suite of:

   Sales ledger
   Purchase ledger
   Nominal ledger
   plus the production of a trial balance and profit and loss account.

2. **Sage Accountant**
   Added to the Bookkeeper programs are:

   Balance sheets
   Budgetary control
   Credit control facilities (inc. statements and debt chasing letters)
   Password control
   Year to date turnover figures
   Recurring Bank Payments (e.g. Standing Orders)
   and journal entries
   Depreciation
   Prepayments and Accruals
   Writing off bad debts.

3. **Accountant Plus**
   This includes (as well as the above)

   Stock control and the production of invoices automatically from the stock files (with automatic update of the sales and nominal ledger accounts and of the stock account).

4. Financial Controller

This is the totally integrated version (of the above) and includes additional features such as:

Order processing
Inventory management and accounting.

NOTES

NOTES

NOTES

NOTES